Is This All There Is?

5 changes to rejuvenate
your company

Kerry Tucker, Teresa Siles
& Blake Tucker Nelson

 FriesenPress

One Printers Way
Altona, MB R0G 0B0
Canada

www.friesenpress.com

ISBN
978-1-03-912850-7 (Hardcover)
978-1-03-912849-1 (Paperback)
978-1-03-912851-4 (eBook)

1. BUSINESS & ECONOMICS, ORGANIZATIONAL DEVELOPMENT

Distributed to the trade by The Ingram Book Company

This is a book about knowledge accumulated over a lifetime of leadership by the leaders of the San Diego-based public relations firm Nuffer, Smith, Tucker, Inc. It's a book of the "tried and true" systems that, over time, have repeatedly led planning teams to the discovery of new opportunities to refresh or rejuvenate a company, trade association, or not-for-profit community group.

Dedication

Fly home La Paloma Linda

Table of Contents

Prologue

by Kerry Tucker

Is this all there is? I remember this reoccurring thought as if it were yesterday—not fifty years ago.

I'd gone to college with modest aspirations. Make no mistake about it, I was after the American Dream, and college was my pathway. Beyond that, the road was foggy. My parents didn't push me to go to college as other moms and dads did. The reality is they didn't have to. Looming over any young man's head in the 1960s was Vietnam. The choices were stay in school, face the draft, or join the reserves. I stayed in school and joined the Air Force Reserves.

My military obligation was complete by my mid-twenties. I had a beautiful wife and a wonderful little girl. I had some early professional wins under my belt and began collecting the trappings of success—a new home, swimming pool, new cars, and a boat docked at Folsom Lake.

Life seemed relatively easy. Any challenge seemed within reach. Yet in the back of my head two questions lingered: Is this really all there is? Have I really earned a chair at the adult table next Easter? The short answer was "no." I liked the amenities all right, but at that point in my life, I had no idea of the power of passion focused on purpose, impassioned leaders fueling others on value-driven issues making a difference for a company, an industry, a community, a country, even the world.

As we pondered how to celebrate our fifty years of life as a business, a colleague asked what seemed at the time like simple questions: "What have you learned? Can others learn from a handful of your greatest discoveries?" They seem simple questions until you think of them in the context of making a difference in someone's life.

What is your definition of business success? Think about it for a moment. An answer, for many people, is tied to profitability on some level. But with all due respect to the warriors who bring home the bacon every day, year after year—"Is this all there is?" Is financial prosperity the only measure of success to which we hold ourselves accountable?

We would argue that individual prosperity isn't enough to be deemed "successful." For companies, profitability is table stakes in order to do something even more significant: create a purposeful organization.

The world today is like none other in history. Americans feel a growing sense of pessimism about economic opportunity and the prospect of upward mobility—the very bedrock of the American Dream. The gap between the "haves" and the "have-nots" is expanding, with the rich getting richer and the poor getting poorer; something our friend and colleague, sociologist Larry Kaagan has been warning us about for decades.

Every day, Americans are frustrated with their plight in life—demanding change in how traditional institutions, like government, media, and business meet the needs of society. Trust has eroded across traditional institutions.

Consumers, especially younger segments, want to know what brands, companies, and industries are doing to make the world a better place—above and beyond enjoying economic vitality. Prosperity opens the door to allow organizations to invest in social improvements. Purpose-driven strategies go a long way to rebuilding public trust in organizations like yours and mine.

As a company leader, your definition of success should serve as the North Star of your organization. It should weave into every decision you make, project you take on, and person you hire.

A recipe for defining your business's success normally includes a mix of following your passions and careful planning for the future, with a sprinkle of serendipity. It's a mix of asking questions and making decisions that align stakeholders, especially employees, behind your company purpose and vision. It's a commitment to doing what's right in life and knowing that it's possible to thrive personally and professionally at the same time. By no means do we have it all figured out, but we've made some good headway that we want to share and that we believe will make you a better leader, manager, or CEO.

This is a book about knowledge accumulated over a lifetime of leadership by the founders and CEOs of Nuffer, Smith, Tucker, Inc., a San Diego-based public relations firm that has been a leader in issue management and strategic planning for more than five decades. These learnings reflect decades of polishing, refining and, simplifying complex business systems to improve performance. It's not a "one and done" account of a trendy new idea, which may or may not stand the test of time. This is a book of the "tried and true" systems that over time have repeatedly led CEOs and planning teams to the discovery of new opportunities to refresh or rejuvenate a company, trade association, or not-for-profit community group.

This is a book designed for constructive use of airplane time. In the hours it takes to fly from Los Angeles to Washington National, leaders from any walk of life can take a fresh, uninterrupted look at what the authors have gleaned from fifty years of consulting for organizations.

This book includes just enough description to allow you to investigate and/or delegate to one of your lieutenants a deeper dive to determine if there's benefit to your organization in pursuing one or more of these learnings as you envision success for your enterprise.

We encourage companies, trade associations, and not-for-profit community groups to evaluate each learning first as a stand-alone candidate for improving performance, and then collectively as a plan pursuing strategic rejuvenation for the future.

For us, the ingredients of success look like this:

1. Make a difference; focus on purpose.

2. Make good with the world; live your values.

3. Don't wait for change; anticipate, manage, and shape it.

4. Set a clear vision and a plan to fulfill it.

5. Align the organization: strategy, culture, infrastructure.

6. Thrive personally and professionally.

What you will find in the subsequent pages is the cumulative thinking of three perspectives from two very different generations.

My daughter, Blake Tucker Nelson, runs My Sage PR, a boutique public affairs firm in Carlsbad, California, and colleague Teresa Siles is president and partner at Nuffer, Smith, Tucker, a twenty-person public-relations firm that bears my name. They are of a similar age and of the generation that grew up wanting much more than a paycheck. Personal fulfillment and meaning beyond the workplace is for them not a luxury, but an expectation. Through our collective lives and work to date, we've become aligned on what matters and we have seen first-hand our efforts drive personal fulfillment and business success.

This is a book that draws from fifty years of learnings from Nuffer, Smith, Tucker, which has represented brands that include the likes of WD-40 Company, McDonald's, Got Milk?, Chicken of the Sea, Green Giant Fresh, and the National Pork Board. It's about our company's founders and the leadership and the culture they began to formally build when the doors opened five decades ago.

Agriculture is the firm's first niche, and our long history in that arena gives us unique insights applicable to any industry or business type. After all, agriculture today is not what it used to be. It's dynamic, complex, increasingly driven by the marketplace, and competing with an urban population for finite natural resources needed to grow food, fuel, and fiber for our neighbors, our country, and our world.

In the pages to follow, we draw from interviews with a cadre of client CEOs in the agriculture space whom we've come to know and respect. Their stories tell how they put one or more of the five learnings into practice, with much success, and provide real world examples of how you can do the same.

Even if your work is far from the farm, we're confident business leaders—especially from smaller companies or trade groups—will see themselves and their businesses in the stories we tell here and the lessons learned in the process.

This book is dedicated to the late Nuffer, Smith, Tucker founders David Lee Nuffer and Robert Frances Smith, along with Bill Trumpfheller, a student I hired who later went on to lead and own the firm. In addition, we dedicate this book to all those who are intellectually curious: First and foremost, Sharon McNerney, Cynthia Carson, Rus Shortridge, Doris Derelian, M. Robert Reider, Earl Parker, Tanya Johnson, and handful of others who push the cerebral envelope every day. This includes members of our Food Foresight trends panel and the likes of Bill Bishop, Larry Kaagan, Carl Keen, Martha Roberts, Jeff Dlott, Arnott Duncan, Bill Even, Chris Novak, Tim York, Tammy Anderson-Wise, Richard Waycott, Miles Reiter, Jamie Strachan, and Jamie Johnson.

At the time of this writing, it's been ten years since I sold the company to my protégé and friend Bill Trumpfheller. Since then, I've been transitioning our robust agri-food clientele from the clutches of this grizzly veteran to Teresa. Teresa, like Blake, is smarter than I could ever be, and with that gift comes an obligation far greater than I could make on my own. Their growth is the ultimate in leveraging the concept of giving back.

The last five years—even the forty-five before—has a warp speed about them. Another five will soon come and go. In a dramatic turn for our company, Bill Trumpfheller died suddenly late in December of 2016, leaving his wife and daughters. Life stops just enough to say goodbye with a promise to never forget.

Teresa and two colleagues, Price Adams and Mary Correia Moreno, now own the firm and are experiencing the changing dynamics and organizational growth that we often counsel clients through. She's putting to a personal test the lessons outlined here.

Learning 1

Make a Difference; Focus on Purpose

"I have one life and one chance to make it count for something…
My faith demands that I do whatever I can, wherever I am,
whenever I can, for as long as I can with whatever I have
to try to make a difference."
—Jimmy Carter

The heart and soul of Nuffer, Smith, Tucker lies with company founders David Lee Nuffer and Robert Frances Smith, and those who followed later with common purpose, values, and a vision for the future. Their focus is on the end benefit they provide to people or society at large.

Their unwavering commitment to make a difference in this world for their families, their businesses, and their communities is well documented in the pages that follow. Intrinsically, they saw an expanded interpretation of success and knew that a commitment to a purposeful life through business and personal dedication was one—if not, the most important—thing we can do as human beings.

Purpose taps into our deep-rooted desires to create meaning and has been the purview of existential philosophers and deep thinkers alike since the beginning of time. More recently, the concept of organizational purpose moved to the C-suite, as companies that connect with consumers on reasons for existence beyond the mighty dollar tend to thrive—and, paradoxically, see soaring profits to boot. Many of the best-performing financial companies are purpose-driven companies.

A lot has been written about the millennial generation—born roughly between the early 1980s and the early 2000s—including commentary on a work ethic. Articles on how to work with millennials are plentiful. In our experience, one of the best ways to motivate and inspire millennials is to align them behind purposeful work.

Forward-looking organizations are adding their purpose to their company's fundamental assets: mission, vision, values, and brand positioning.

Such disparate brands as IBM, Jack Daniel's, and Google have been cited as purposeful brands. These companies and others are gaining a competitive edge by defining what they stand for with purpose and values that transcend gender, demographics, politics, and other factors that tend to divide rather than unite. We call them "purpose-driven" organizations.

Today, Nuffer, Smith, Tucker finds itself helping businesses of all types uncover their own purpose.

Tucker Tales

> *Following a couple of years of warm-up working with a minor league professional football team and a small but influential lobbying outfit, I landed at Dairy Council of California. It didn't take me long to figure out the organization was not just about selling milk. Sure, milk was part of the mix, but it became clear to me that Dairy Council of California saw its role as something larger and more significant than spin doctors for cheese and yogurt.*
>
> *There was, and continues to be, a higher calling at work for Dairy Council of California. It's a "cause" that goes back more than a century, when the organization was founded by California dairy*

families and local milk bottlers. It's a cause that educators, health professionals, and the dairy industry can collectively get behind. That cause is not to sell milk, but rather something far more meaningful: to elevate the health and wellness of children and families through lifelong eating patterns. It was at Dairy Council of California that I first saw the power of purpose to motivate me and others.

Purpose: Brand ideals with a pinch of altruism

For many organizations, purpose is now the foundation upon which everything else can and should be built, and the benefits are more than altruism. Developing a purpose statement is hard work. You must ask yourself the tough questions about why you do what you do. In addition, you need to think through whether or not that purpose is in fact authentic. Are you walking the talk or is the purpose only words on paper? Purpose statements should be checked for authenticity, and business leaders should question what others—including activists and opponents—may think when hearing a company's purpose. Those that can pass the sniff test can reap rewards.

The pandemic has accelerated corporate focus on purpose, according to a story in PRovoke Media[1]. Hannah Peters, executive vice president at WE, says purpose is not just about doing the right thing or morality but rather materiality. "There's a clear business case for purpose… Companies are taking a stand and acting with purpose because they have a responsibility to employees and stakeholders to be viable and to do things that maintain their license to operate…"

Jim Stengel, previous Global Marketing Officer for Proctor & Gamble, is among many business leaders eyeing purpose-driven enterprises. Stengel conducted a ten-year study on more than 50,000 brands and found those that focused on what he calls "brand ideals" outperformed others. In fact, the top fifty highest-performing companies

---

1 Maja Pawinska Sims, "PRovokeNA: How Leaders Are Innovating In Real Time To Lead With Purpose," PRovoke Media, February 25, 2021, https://www.provokemedia.com/latest/article/provoke-na-how-leaders-are-innovating-in-real-time-to-lead-with-purpose

(dubbed "Stengel 50") grew three times faster than their competitors, and an investment in the Stengel 50 would have been 400 percent more profitable than an investment in the S&P 500. In addition to financial success, purpose-driven organizations also score high marks for creating engagement, cultivating workplace satisfaction, and even eliciting happiness. We've seen it work firsthand for Fortune 500 companies and mom-and-pop shops alike.

A clearly defined purpose, combined with a thoughtful look at the world around you and a plan to achieve your vision are the foundational elements of success. Meanwhile, let's address the role of passion, which often goes hand-in-hand with purpose.

The role of passion is to drive purpose

Angela Duckworth, in her book *Grit*, cites the parable of a bricklayer. When asked what they are doing, three bricklayers give varying answers:

- The first says, "I'm laying bricks."

- The second says, "I'm building a church."

- The third says, "I am building the house of God."

The first has a job. The second has a career. The third has a purpose-driven calling.

Some people use the terms passion and purpose interchangeably, but they are different and, when aligned, can catapult people and businesses to extraordinary heights.

Passion by definition is a powerful inner feeling that grabs you and emotionally charges your pursuit of something or someone. Some call passion a step short of crazy. Simply put, your passion drives your personal fulfillment.

Scott Cohen, email marketing strategist and creator of the blog *Scott Writes Everything*, writes, "Passion is like energy. You can't teach it, but you can cultivate and harness it. While not everyone is blessed with passion, one individual can set the tone for an entire company of people because of the cause of that one leader."

Passion cannot be taught, but it can serve as the spark that keeps your company true to its purpose. As a company leader, your passion will be key to your success in more ways than one:

1. Passion is infectious. It breeds enthusiasm. If you have the right team, it will travel through them.

2. Passion will get stronger in the good times and give you the strength to keep going through the bad.

3. Passion can guide your hiring process. You are looking for people who share crazy qualities and embrace what you are trying to build for the greater good.

Tucker Tales

As I grew more focused in my work with Dairy Council of California, that familiar feeling of euphoria appeared frequently the same way it did following the rendition of "Johnny B. Goode" by Joe Walsh or seeing my son's walk off homerun in his final game as a professional ballplayer.

- *It was unleashed at a meeting in Boston where the country's leading chefs and health professionals agreed on the importance of marrying taste and health to promote that all foods can fit in a healthful diet.*

- *It was there in Sacramento, at a meeting of more than 200 California agricultural commodities, when consensus was facilitated on a platform of priorities that the state's farmers and ranchers agreed to work together on. There was only one other time in recent history that California agriculture could agree on anything ("Big Green" voter proposition).*

- *It was there in San Diego the day Southern California Edison announced it was calling off merger talks with San Diego Gas*

& Electric Company (due to resistance from a Nuffer, Smith, Tucker-driven coalition of San Diego community leaders).

Agriculture—well suited to connect on purpose

In our view, there could be no better sector suited to uncover and share its purpose than agriculture. After all, food—healthy and sustainably produced food—is the foundation not only for health and wellness, but also for allowing people and societies at large to thrive.

In 2016, the California State Board of Food and Agriculture turned to Nuffer, Smith, Tucker to facilitate an update to its strategic plan, dubbed Ag Vision. Armed with a belief in purpose-driven organizations, Nuffer, Smith, Tucker guided the board through a process to define the purpose for California agriculture.

The end result was the following purpose statement:

California agriculture is making California a better place to live because of what we grow and how we grow it.

In developing this statement of purpose for agriculture, we collected industry input on benefits and chronicled them into this plan (via interviews, electronic survey, planning sessions). Those benefits are intricately woven into the purpose statement, with each piece of the statement rich with meaning. Consider this:

- California agriculture is "making California a better place to live" through its contributions to the economy, landscape, food system, and, importantly, way of life. Many we spoke with talked about the passionate, hard-working farm families behind California agriculture and the role they play in their communities and beyond.

- "What we grow" speaks to the diversity of California agriculture. In fact, "diverse" is the term we heard most often in describing California agriculture. California is home to farming operations of all sizes: livestock and specialty crops, permanent and annual crops, and conventional and organic farms. This diversity is all part of the story of "what we grow." Also inherent in this is the idea that California farmers and ranchers are doing more than producing food—they are producing nourishment and fuel for both individuals and societies to advance.

• We also heard that California growers are on the leading edge of innovation, setting the standard on environmental stewardship and taking great care in how they grow, thus supporting the importance of the "how we grow it" part of the purpose statement. Also critical is the spirit of the farm families who grow and market California food and agricultural products.

Sustainable practices and climate change are enjoying phenomenal attention, therefore providing another opportunity for agriculture to demonstrate its purpose. For instance, on the same day in 2021, government officials—led by both President Joe Biden and California Governor Gavin Newsom—announced a slew of climate actions that promise to make sustainable farming practices and climate change major federal and state priorities for years to come.

Other examples of purpose at work with agriculture come from Simpatica, the largest avocado grower in the U.S., which defines its purpose as improving health and happiness while bringing friends and families together. Still another example comes from the National Association of State Departments of Food and Agriculture's planning session, which saw its purpose as nourishing people and communities while serving as stewards of the environment and public trust.

We can hear what you are thinking: Sure, it might be easy for folks feeding the world to define a "purpose," but what about other types of businesses? How is my business meaningful? Hold tight… we'll get there.

Let your purpose tell your "story"

Agriculture, like most other businesses, is often in the position of wanting to "tell its story" to consumers—particularly in recent years as consumer interest and pressures on the industry intensify. There is a tendency to want to "inform" or "educate" audiences.

How many times have you heard someone say, "We've got to tell our story," or "We just need to make them understand," or "If they could only see the big picture."

There's a big flaw in these assumptions. For the most part, people don't care about your challenges and explanations. While it can be tempting to shout from the rooftops about how great your organization is, there is a better, more meaningful way: let your purpose be your story.

As we write this learning, mistrust of business, politics, and nearly all traditional institutions is thick in the air with American consumers, particularly millennials. But purpose-driven brands and companies are doing well and garnering public trust in a time when trust has been on a downward spiral. So, after clearly defining your social purpose, sharing it through storytelling can be a powerful tool, particularly in today's world of information overload where any and everyone has a voice, and the platforms in which to share it are plentiful and growing. The sheer volume of ideas accessible online and the velocity in which information—whether true or false—can be shared have created an environment where it is difficult to break through the clutter and build a brand.

In addition, various studies show Americans tend to self-select information sources, and people tend to gravitate toward information sources that support their viewpoint. Appeals to reason and logic— particularly when it comes to issues that are central to our identity and our moral principles—often fail. Instead, cognitive scientists, behavioral economists, and psychologists believe our brains respond well to stories.

"Humans live in a storm of stories," says Jonathan Gottschall, who wrote *Storytelling Animal: How Stories Make Us Human.*

"We live in stories all day long and dream in stories all night long. We communicate through stories and learn from them. We collapse gratefully into stories after a long day at work. Without personal life stories to organize our experience, our own lives would lack coherence and meaning," Gottschall says in an article on Fast Company.[2]

Sharing your purpose through storytelling is a powerful tool. It allows opportunity to engage in two-way dialogue, listen and respond to public concerns, and foster conversations without getting defensive over public perceptions about your company, industry, or profession.

Storytelling is powerful because people can relate and empathize says those at Social Deck. "They can put themselves in that situation— and recognize the story and the steps toward making a change. They also leverage social norms (showing that if others can do it, 'I can too.' Personal stories demonstrate the small things people can do that are easy, convenient and show the benefits that have come from changing behavior, encouraging others to make the change too."[3]

Beyond purpose: Consumers want companies to take a stand on issues that matter

Beyond articulating a clear purpose and sharing it through storytelling, consumers are now expecting companies to take a stand on issues that matter to them. From climate change to systemic racism and gender equity, companies are being challenged to take a stand—and back it up with actions.

The killing of George Floyd sparked a growing collective awareness of systemic and deep-rooted racism across American life. While many were focused on police reform, American businesses of all types had their feet held to the fire on where they stand on racial injustice— and it didn't stop there. From boardroom representation to actions to demonstrate espoused claims of diversity, public demands were loud and clear. The end result was increased accountability across the board

---

2   Jonathan Gottschall, "The Science of Storytelling: How Narrative Cuts Through Distraction Like Nothing else," Fast Company, October 16, 2013, https://www.fastcompany.com/3020044/the-science-of-storytelling-how-narrative-cuts-through-distraction

3   Kate Bowmaker, "Storytelling and Behaviour Change," Social Deck, accessed January 14, 2021, https://www.thesocialdeck.com.au/blog/storytelling-and-behaviour-change

for all businesses to promote diversity, equity, and inclusion in policy and—most importantly—practice and action.

What is likely to be permanent for corporate decisionmakers, government officials, and even organized religion is the risk of losing business—and even the ability to function at all—if the issues of new and sometimes different stakeholders are not addressed. If there is any doubt about the importance of adopting policies and practices that are in alignment with changing social expectations, one need look no further than companies that have bucked the trend in downward trust levels. Companies that not only use the language of social responsibility, but which also "walk the talk" and adopt socially responsible practices (think of the clothing brand Patagonia) are able to consolidate fierce consumer loyalty and wider societal acclaim all at the same time.

Teresa and Blake's Take

We first started integrating purpose into our planning efforts around 2015. At the time, it was new thinking—and terminology—that caught attention. Since then, the word "purpose" has become common vernacular in the business community. With that, we've seen our fair share of purpose-washing going on. What some companies fail to realize is that developing your purpose statement is the easy part—it's living it that is a challenge. Words like sustainable, transparent, trust, and honesty are powerful terms to communicate your purpose, as long as you commit to backing it up. Avoid trending buzzwords unless they are at the core of your company. You want your company's purpose to stand the test of time, so avoid pandering to lightning-rod topics of the moment. The savvy, and especially the young, can see right through efforts that are inauthentic, shallow or, in the worst-case scenario, designed to deceive. Authenticity is the key, and actions—not just words—are what build trust.

Get to work: An exercise on uncovering your purpose

How do you define your organizational purpose? For some organizations—particularly not-for-profit groups and public agencies—the purpose can be very clear. For others, it requires a little digging. Consider the following questions and write down your answers.

- What is the end benefit of your company, product, or service to society at large? Think beyond your customers, consumers, and employees.

- What's your history? How and why did you come to be?

- Would anyone care if your company went away? If so, why?

- How does what you do improve people's lives?

- Why is it important to the people you serve?

- Why does your existence matter?

Review your work and pen a short, concise statement that focuses on what you believe your company contributes to society as a whole. From there, ask yourself these questions:

- Does the statement describe the end benefit to people or society as a whole or narrow down to one stakeholder group, like customers? If it's narrow, broaden your thinking. Push yourself.

- Is it clear, compelling, memorable, and in need of little explanation?

- Is it inspirational, a catalyst for team spirit?

- Can your organization walk this talk? How can it demonstrate its purpose in action?

- Where are the vulnerabilities in this purpose?

- How will you share your purpose through storytelling?

Learning 2

Make Good With the World; Live Your Values

"Never, never, never give up"
— Winston Churchill

Core values are the timeless philosophical guidelines that drive decisions of an organization from top to bottom, side to side. They stem from what the founders and/or top management envision as the top five (or more) principles that drive decisions and comprise the heart and soul of any company, community group or trade association.

An explicit set of core values gives employees guidance on how top management expects them to behave. Values are also used to recruit (and reward) employees likely to be a good fit for your organization.

The most powerful core values are those that not only serve a company but also the communities in which that company does business.

Gaining clarity of values up front, especially if there are conflicts early on, can help identify and achieve consensus on thorny principles that need a philosophical foundation.

Nuffer, Smith, Tucker is a values-driven company. Values are talked about often, and it's not uncommon to hear them brought up in everyday conversation. The principles below, with the exception of a few minor word changes, have been in place for several years. They include:

1. Help people discover things they wouldn't see on their own.

2. Make a difference with the cards you're dealt.

3. Do what's right -- right is right, wrong is wrong.

4. Deliver on your commitments.

5. Be candid but know when to back off and be supportive.

6. Be respectful of other points of view.

7. Balance hard work, fun, and the needs of each individual.

Values and ethics: Doing what's right

Doing "what's right" as a company became the last core value put to paper at Nuffer, Smith, Tucker. It was one the company tried to live by even though it took years to formalize as a core value. It was only after we tried—unsuccessfully—to develop an ethics policy that it was added as a value. The ethics policy effort was futile in that each principle we outlined felt obvious and rudimentary. From there, we had numerous discussions about that gut instinct inherent in us all about what's right and what's wrong.

Even a child instinctively knows right from wrong. You can see it in grandchildren testing grandma's reaction before making a run at the freezer for the third ice cream sandwich of the day. It's that little voice in the back of your head that signals right from wrong. It doesn't have to get much deeper than that. We're born with a conscience, and it distinguishes right and wrong if we listen.

One of our management team brethren argued against the "do what's right" core value because he believed different people could interpret right and wrong in different ways. After several years of debate, we finally agreed that employees hired for their skill and values set had enough in common to be encouraged to listen to and act on their conscience. Our long-time client WD-40 Company framed their commitment this way: "We value doing the right thing." We ended up adopting similar language.

Tucker Tales

> When I first came to town in 1980, Nuffer, Smith, Tucker was eager to grow. We felt that by offering pro bono strategic planning expertise, we could not only make a difference, but also positively position the firm. While it was a significant investment in time, it was well known among community leaders that Nuffer, Smith, Tucker was offering pro bono professional services. Through our support, companies and groups reached new levels of effectiveness and efficiencies that community leaders appreciated. Demonstrating value to a room full of potential clients was phenomenally successful and helped both the community and the company.

It's one thing to say we do what's right; it's quite another in practice. On occasion, we've parted ways with clients we believed were on the wrong side of right. We walked away from the Red Cross when we couldn't convince its CEO that it was in the best interest of the institution and the community for her to resign; Nuffer, Smith, Tucker was later rehired when the CEO was removed.

In another example, we walked away from a client who repeatedly abused our staff to tears on what became an almost daily occurrence. Right is right and wrong is wrong, and that was wrong. We exhausted all attempts to fix this ugly situation and ended up leaving behind $60,000 in fees owed to us. Resolving the issue would have meant "outing" an influential CEO with sensitive ties to another large client. We took a big gulp, kicked ourselves for letting greed slow down the inevitable decision, and moved on.

Another example of a values-driven company is The Wonderful Company. Wonderful is a privately held $5 billion company that "grows, harvests, bottles, and markets a diverse range of healthy products including, fruits, nuts, flowers, waters, wines, and juices." (www. wonderful.com/press)

Stewart Resnick is the hard-driving, fiercely competitive billionaire businessman who, with his wife, Lynda, owns a suite of companies under The Wonderful Company brand. Resnick companies play to win. Resnick is as shrewd as they come. His companies dominate or intend to dominate the industries and markets in which they play. He is known for the quality of people he surrounds himself with and their ability to create a culture to meet his ambitious financial objectives.

The Resnicks are investing millions upon millions of dollars building The Wonderful Company brand in an agri-food sector that can count its consumer brands with any significant recognition on one hand.

Generous investments by the Resnicks are well known in education, sustainability, and philanthropy circles, showing the company's values don't just live in an employee handbook somewhere—they are used to articulate what the company stands for and to guide decisions and actions by the company and its leadership.

A closer look: The Wonderful Company values

We believe there is an incredible power in The Wonderful family of brands to inspire healthier choices and to support our communities. By helping nourish our neighbors with high-quality, healthy products, we believe we can grow a better world. Their four values include:

1. **"We act differently**—with courage and fearlessness, we are relentless in our quest to inspire healthier food and beverage choices... as a privately held organization, we have the freedom and the power to make quick and effective decisions.

2. **"We are harvesting a better world**—we use the power of business to make the world a better place.

3. **"We play to win**—our employees set ambitious goals and meet challenges with unified purpose and unmatched energy.

4. **"We nourish naturally**—we believe that what you put into your body matters. The most nutritious—and best tasting—foods are those from nature."

Humility: The unwritten principle

At Nuffer, Smith, Tucker, humility is an unwritten value shared and treasured by our founders and today's leadership. It's a value that may be difficult to adopt company-wide, but that—if done well—can be important to creating a culture poised for success.

There are periods in our history when confidence crossed the line of arrogance and humility danced in and out of our company culture. Arrogance—and the self-importance it breeds—is the antithesis of "selfless" humility.

Dave Nuffer captures an undertone that is evident in the halls at Nuffer, Smith, Tucker headquarters. In his novel, *Defeat Is a Natural Habit* (unpublished), he wrote, "Resolved, that all members do their inspired best to step down hard on arrogance and all the misery it creates."

Some academics now formally link humility to performance improvements. A collaborative organizational culture tends to follow humble leaders. Margaret Mayo, professor of Leadership and Organizational Behavior at IE Business School in Madrid, says, "The world becomes a better place when we choose humble, unassuming people as our leaders."

Tucker Tales

Bob Smith intuitively captured the essence of selfless leadership, as did Dave Nuffer, but they approached it in different ways.

Dave never separated himself too far from his desert roots or his friends south of the border. He loved Mexico, its people, the mariachi music, and bullfights, and his home in Ensenada. He returned to the small town of El Centro a couple of times a year, occasionally to help city fathers address threats to water, the region's lifeblood. Dave graduated from University of Redlands, a small private liberal arts college, and walked away from graduate school at University of California under protest. He left behind his still-unfinished thesis.

While his presence in the San Diego business community was bigger than life itself—he was the go-to guy to get something done in San Diego—Dave was humbled frequently along life's pathway, not the least of which was his experience with his unpublished novel, Defeat Is a Natural Habit.

After hiring a Hollywood agent and rewriting it several times, he turned his interests to tracking down haunts of Ernest Hemingway around the world. He and I traveled from Ketchum to Key West to Paris to Havana. Nuffer wrote two books with unusual insights into Hemingway's world. He also authored a book on the history of Imperial Valley.

Bob on the other hand, graduated from University of Southern California via the Navy's ROTC program before receiving an MBA from UCLA—light years from the Imperial Valley desert. Nonetheless, it was Dave—his friend, partner, and neighbor—who captured the essence of Bob when he wrote:

"From the moment of that first handshake, I—along with countless others I am sure—knew he was different, a cut above. Name any adjective that describes an unusual man and it fit Bob Smith, and you knew that instinctively and instantly.

"Bob had an almost biblical belief in people. He knew that every one of us was doing his or her best, and he trusted us implicitly, and if that trust was ever betrayed, he never commented on it. His influence was felt in many places around the globe, and I don't believe he was ever fired by anyone."

Bob's "always take the high road" style of leadership was an important learning and it remains a way of life at Nuffer, Smith, Tucker.

Giving back to employees and communities

"Giving back" is something many organizations aspire to do. Some do so genuinely, and others do it as a form of "corporate social responsibility."

Nuffer, Smith, Tucker believes strongly in investing resources in growing our people and supporting the communities where we live, work, and play. At the same time, we do so for mutual benefit. We invest where there's the greatest need, and it makes the most sense for growing our company.

We invest generously in community initiatives that support our company purpose and values. This means targeting and investing time and resources in the community groups that wield influence and best support our business plan. It also means investing in professional development for employees.

With the dramatic shifts in demographics—baby boomers moving out and younger segments moving in—finding and keeping employees who match your culture is increasingly difficult, and many would-be employees want to align with organizations that give back in some way.

We learned early on from Nuffer's example of giving back to the local community. He put up with challenges from our advertising firm owner at the time, but he didn't need data to justify supporting the community. Investing resources—both time and money—in downtown San Diego was in his blood, and the firm grew and prospered with his influence in the community.

A closer look: Dave Nuffer

The following is a reflection on our founder by Alex Montoya, born in Colombia with no arms and one leg. Alex is currently a business owner, author, and motivational speaker.

> *When I graduated from Notre Dame and returned to the 619 (San Diego area code), I sent out one hundred resumes with cover letters. I figured I'd get a few back, right? Maybe score a half dozen interviews or so among PR agencies, newspapers,*

and sports teams in town. I got exactly one response. It was from David Nuffer.

*He didn't even have a job available but was willing to meet with me for an "informational interview." I walked into his office on a sunny September day, admiring a Steve Garvey autographed baseball. He asked if I liked baseball. "Of course," I said. He asked who my team was, and when I said the Padres, he said, "Good," and smiled with a grin as bright as his white hair and as plain as his tan face and suit. "I was afraid you'd say the Dodgers. I ***** hate the Dodgers."*

That was Dave, I learned, and I saw his crusty yet humorous ways even more when he offered me a twelve-hour-a-week job. I needed it. I took it.

He swore a lot. He hated the concept of casual Fridays. He shed a tear when one of his clients, The Access Center, offered me a full-time job. He made sure I went to spring training and bought me margaritas. He stayed in touch long after I'd left the company.

One time, he knew then–NFL commissioner Paul Tagliabue would be in town for a luncheon, so he offered to pick me up at home and take me. "Be ready on Sunday at noon," he growled. I was, but Dave never showed. The luncheon was Monday at noon. He picked me up and apologized for twenty minutes.

When, after many years, I achieved my goal to work for the Padres, he cut out the notice in the paper, highlighted it, and inscribed a note and framed both. It read: Paso por paso, se llega lejos… Step by step, we travel miles.

Teresa and Blake's Take

> *We remember it well when the CEO of a San Diego-based, not-for-profit organization saw draft values we had developed—based on insights from their team—during a planning meeting and gave them the rubber stamp. "Those work," she said. "But I know the board doesn't want to spend time on the touchy-feely stuff. Let's get to the meat."*

We were shocked. What our client failed to realize is that while all parts of a strategic plan are important, the values are perhaps the most important. In fact, values should be principles that drive decision making at all levels of the organization and, for that reason, they are worthy of attention. Think of values as the Yellow Brick Road—if you stick to it, it will lead you to the Emerald City, or in this case, your purpose. Current and future employees will gravitate to your values and use them to guide action when they reach a dangerous fork in the road.

Get to work: Uncovering the principles behind decisions

While most companies of significant size have defined values, not all organizations apply them—but they should. Values should be more than words on paper and should drive actions both big and small. Think about what principles you use to drive your decisions.

Once defined, you can get others involved in discussing the core values, which should apply at every level of the organization. Have teams break up into small groups to talk about what the values mean to them.

Best-selling authors, Jim Collins, founder of the Management Laboratory, and Jerry Porras, a professor emeritus at Stanford University, offered the following questions about core values in a seminal article in the Harvard Business Review paper on strategic planning, "Building Your Company's Vision" (September–October 1996). Consider their probes:

- What core values do you personally bring to your work?

- What would you tell your children are the core values that you hold at work and that you hope they will hold when they become working adults?

- If you awoke tomorrow morning with enough money to retire for the rest of your life, would you continue to live those core values?

- Can you envision them being as valid for you 100 years from now as they are today?

- Would you want to hold those core values, even if at some point one or more became a competitive disadvantage?

- If you were to start a new organization tomorrow in a different line of work what core values would you build into the new organization regardless of its industry?

Learning 3

Don't Wait for Change; Anticipate, Manage, and Shape It

*"Never ever depend on governments or institutions
to solve any major problems. All social change comes
from the passion of individuals."*
— Margaret Mead

We've spent most of our adult lives defining and refining systems to anticipate and strategically manage change. Over time, these systems became powerful tools for making a difference in our world. By putting resources—time and dollars—behind top priority issues to accelerate opportunities, redirect threats, and/or make internal adjustments to adapt to change, one can more easily build a purposeful organization.

Most of us handle issues instinctively, almost accidentally—or we wait until they become crises. The issue management process is not about crises. It is summarized by one word: anticipation.

Issue anticipation systems are analogous to establishing radar (even systems of sonar) to help management anticipate and prepare for issues—any condition or pressure that if continued will significantly impact the purpose (or mission) and vision of the enterprise.

An environmental scan of external threats and opportunities is the first step in our strategic planning system, called "Compass." It's also the first step in our issue anticipation model. While we treat the two systems separately, there is overlap and issue management is at the intersection.

Catching issues early in their development, when the strategic options are most plentiful, provides a greater opportunity to cash in on managing change—framing issue conversations, aligning stakeholder support, and shaping how change unfolds. By taking the time to look ahead, one finds the greatest opportunities to strategically advance as a company—even change the game to match competitive advantage.

In a world where information is increasingly socialized and everyone has the opportunity to have a voice on countless platforms, every issue begs for attention. It's easy to get distracted and seduced into allotting precious resources to the wrong issues or to winding down pathways that aren't strategic to an organization's long-term success.

Tools for issue management

While Nuffer, Smith, Tucker sets up systems unique to each client for its issue management programs, any business can benefit from a system that involves the steps in the diagram on pages 32-33. The following illustration is a model developed to help visualize the issue anticipation process—from issue prioritization to the decision to act or not act to facilitating change.

Another way of framing strategy

Kurt Lewin, recognized as the "founder of social psychology," created Force Field Analysis. It is a useful process for thinking through an issue (see Figure 2). Lewin theorized that any level of performance is affected by a field of forces driving both for and against it. Actual performance is the point of equilibrium between the two. Performance can be improved by setting priorities across the field—focusing on the forces on either side with the most influence.

The produce industry, organized by the Produce Marketing Association in partnership with the National Restaurant Association and the International Foodservice Distributors Association, met twice in two years to create a collaborative action plan among stakeholders to double consumption of fruits and vegetables served at foodservice. The group used a Force Field Analysis diagram to evaluate issues and opportunities.

Continuum of Influence

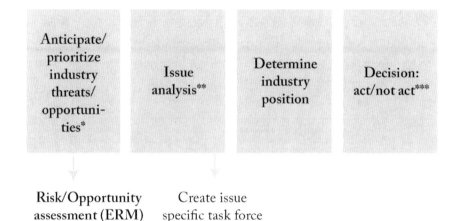

Anticipate/ prioritize industry threats/ opportuni- ties*	Issue analysis**	Determine industry position	Decision: act/not act***

Risk/Opportunity assessment (ERM)

Create issue specific task force

Strategic plan

Share information/ engage industry stakeholders in issue discussions

*Set priorities based on impact on purpose and vision

**Define the issue, identify the stakeholders/likely positions/behavioral inclinations identify likely partners to shape the issue, identify forces working for and against you, draw assumptions of where the issue is headed with no intervention.

***Put research/education plan in place and collaborate where needed to be a) proactive – accelerate opportunity, redirect threat, and/or adjust industry practices - and/or b) reactive with crisis response plan to respond when needed.

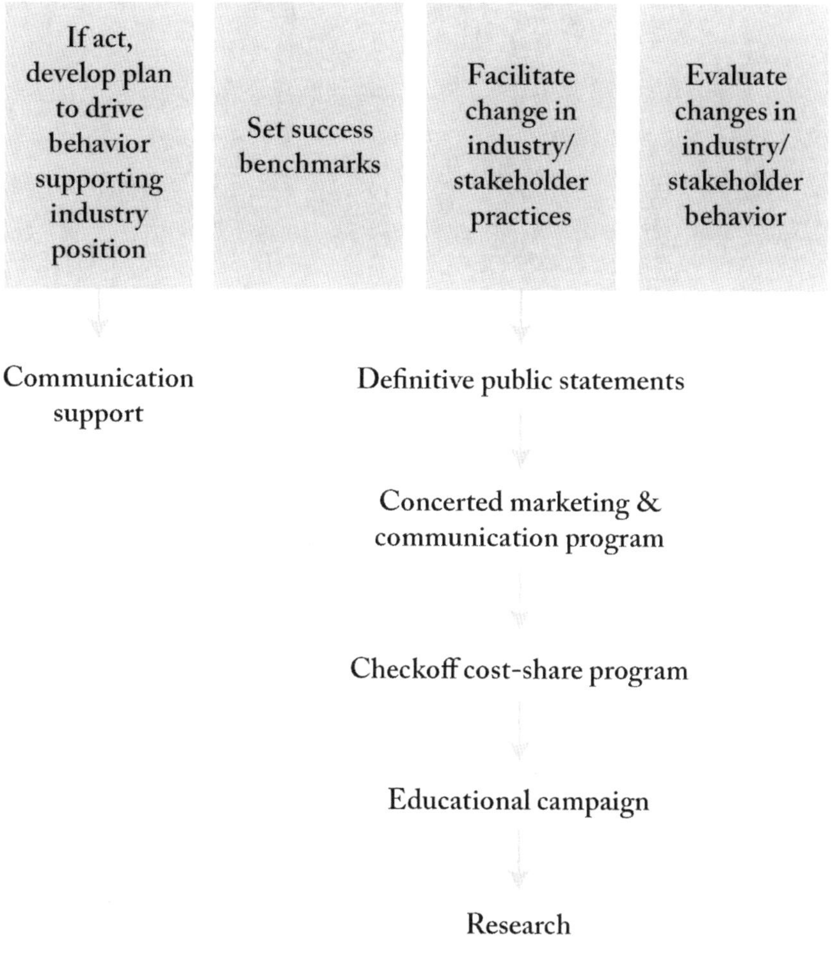

| If act, develop plan to drive behavior supporting industry position | Set success benchmarks | Facilitate change in industry/ stakeholder practices | Evaluate changes in industry/ stakeholder behavior |

Communication support

Definitive public statements

Concerted marketing & communication program

Checkoff cost-share program

Educational campaign

Research

Figure 1: Model of continuum of influence designed to help visualize the issue anticipation process – from prioritization to the decision to act or not to facilitate change

Executive Think Tank: Produce Opportunities in Foodservice

Consensus on Priority Forces

A force field graphically displays external forces that are impacting the achievement of an objective. In this case, upward moving arrows are forces that could increase the use of fresh produce in foodservice and downward moving arrows can be obstacles to achieving that objective.

Forces Working Against Us

There isn't enough collaboration between sectors

R&D is fractionalized; R&D with limited innovation and is currently focused on operations vs. the consumer

Increased use of fresh produce in foodservice

Social responsibility/ sustainability can be positives to build on (there are vulnerabilities too)

Flavor/seasonality/ freshness/quality/best practices around the world offer customer and consumer strengths

Forces Working In Our Favor

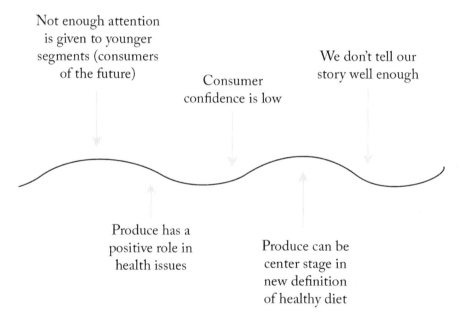

Not enough attention is given to younger segments (consumers of the future)

Consumer confidence is low

We don't tell our story well enough

Produce has a positive role in health issues

Produce can be center stage in new definition of healthy diet

Figure 2: Produce Marketing Association force field analysis

A closer look: Food Foresight

Food Foresight is an issue anticipation and management system for the agri-food chain first developed by Dairy Council of California. Nuffer, Smith, Tucker later adapted the system and applied it more broadly for a variety of agricultural partners. Partners invest in the system that works like this:

- **Media scan/data run**—More than twenty issue categories, from air quality to weight control, are tracked over a six-month period. Traditional media, social media, academic journals, the work of NGO groups, and more are scanned, and articles are collected and assembled into a database.

- **Food Foresight meeting**—The information is scanned and evaluated by a blue-ribbon panel representing various facets of the agri-food industry—from retail to foodservice, production agriculture, health care, food safety, economics, and even the social sciences. The makeup of the panel is extremely important as it provides both a wealth of expertise and a diversity of perspectives—both essential to providing a thorough external analysis. Over a two-and-a-half-day meeting, the panel reviews the scan and begins to outline trends likely to impact the agri-food chain.

- **Trends substantiation/validation**—Following the meeting, further research is done to ensure the trends can be substantiated and validated. This is critical to ensuring the results of the meeting are rooted in indicators in the environment.

- **Development of a Food Foresight report**—A report is then written outlining key trends, implications for the agri-food marketplace, and questions for partner consideration. This report becomes a foundation for strategic planning.

Examples of capitalizing on change

The agri-food sector is moving and changing fast. The result is that the industry must look around and anticipate, shape, and manage change like never before. Those who do will thrive. Those who don't may go the way of the dodo bird. Here are a few examples of clients whose eye toward the future has paid off.

Dairy Council of California

The dairy industry was the first of our clients to realize the power in anticipating and managing change. One of its early successes dealt with a then little-known bone disease (osteoporosis) that scientists found could be prevented with consumption of calcium-rich foods. By identifying this issue early on, Dairy Council of California was able to partner with the American Society for Bone and Mineral Research (ASBMR). Dairy Council of California was interested in promoting the importance of calcium-rich foods. ASBMR was interested in building a case for osteoporosis research. It was a match made in heaven, and together the team was able to raise awareness about this important issue. This resulted in a *Newsweek* cover story and widespread public attention.

The Almond Board of California

The Almond Board of California uncovered new nutrition research emerging in Food Foresight that would, with the industry's help, build a science-based case that repositioned nuts from "bad" foods to "good" foods because of their good fat portfolio. With investments in research and education, the Almond Board helped accelerate this new thinking to the marketplace.

The Produce Marketing Association

The Produce Marketing Association retained Nuffer, Smith, Tucker to do an analysis on a growing number of lethal foodborne illness incidents affecting produce. The report laid a foundation for assessing and shoring up vulnerabilities in the systems in place. A buyer-seller coalition was organized by Tim York, formerly with Markon Cooperative, to accelerate a new safety system for lettuce and leafy greens. Western Growers, under CEO Tom Nassif, led the development of the new safety system and founded the Leafy Greens Marketing Agreement to manage it. To research unanswered questions, Nuffer, Smith, Tucker put three clients together—Produce Marketing Association, Markon Cooperative, and the University of California, Davis—to create the Center for Produce Safety. These actions allowed the produce industry the opportunity to continue to grow demand while advancing its purpose of providing healthy, nutritious—and safe—food to a consuming public.

Creating behavior change

After analyzing issues and determining your desired end game for stakeholders, you may find yourself wondering: How do we get people to take action in support of our position? That's where the behavioral framework comes into play. The behavioral framework is the foundation for the textbook penned by Kerry Tucker, Doris Derelian, PhD, a behavioral psychologist; and Donna Rouner, PhD, a public relations professor at Colorado State University.

At its zenith, Public Relations Writing was adopted by about one hundred colleges and universities around the world. The crux of the theories behind the book and behavioral framework is that people normally resist change and have challenges transforming information to behavior without help. With proper work, however, communication strategies, messages, and tactics can break through the clutter by comparing and contrasting existing behavior with the desired behavior, facilitating discomfort with existing behavior, and offering help in adopting a new behavior.

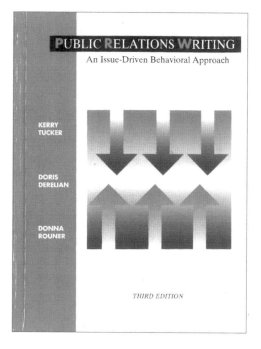

Figure 3: Public Relations Writing: An Issue Driven Behavioral Approach (1996)

The mental route to behavior change

It helps to have a basic understanding of the path a successful message takes to change behavior. There are five basic steps:

1. The message is transferred to personal, real-life needs, concerns, or interests. Before we can react to a message, we must be able to imagine how it will affect us in our own life situation. Connections to real-life situations capture attention for the message.

2. The intent to act is triggered by an individual's own analysis of perceived benefits and consequences. This step represents the big leap between receiving a message and being motivated to do something about it. The intent to act or to form an attitude is initiated here.

3. The message is processed against past experience and perceived expectations of success or failure, and behavioral decisions (to act or

not to act) are made. Once we are motivated to consider action, past experiences and associations are considered, and then behaviors are selected to respond to the message stimuli.

4. Behavior change occurs. Acting on the message is by trial at first. The first action is taken, thought forms complete, evaluation is conducted, and belief is organized. Sometimes, several repetitions occur during this action initiation phase while analyzing the experience from each trial action or thought. Actions taken provide a level of belief about the need, concern, or interest and its behavioral solution.

5. Values and attitudes are formed. The trial actions form an experimental memory that, upon evaluation, produces a positive or negative belief. Positive values and attitudes for the behavior encourage repetition of the cycle; negative values and attitudes discourage it.[4]

Ready to apply the behavioral framework? For each issue around which you would like to create action, consider the following four questions that are the foundation for the behavioral model:

- How can our communication raise a need, concern, or interest to this stakeholder group?

- Is your desired behavior clearly and credibly packaged to meet the need, resolve the concern, or satisfy the interest?

- Have you clearly presented the benefits of action and the consequences of inaction? Have you made the strongest case you can to create discomfort with existing behavior?

- Have you helped the receiver mentally rehearse the desired behavior?

---

4 A note from Doris Derelian, PH. D. on evaluation: Social scientists now point to evidence that after the initial or secondary application of a new behavior, evaluation kicks in to process and value the intended behavior. If positive, the behavior is repeated. If negative, the behavior is scrubbed and not likely to be repeated. This is done at lightning speed, often without conscious thought or verbalization. What we call "learning" is the accumulation of your memory of those actions and your respective value for the behavior.

Applying these principles and packaging communications in this manner will provide you with the best opportunity to elicit the desired behavior from decision makers (e.g., public and private policymakers, stakeholders, customers, and even consumers).

While the behavioral framework may appear to be a vast, oversimplification of the complexity of the communications process, its principles are borrowed from theory describing successful learning. Most successful public relations campaigns are, in fact, based on the implicit use of these concepts.

Nuffer, Smith, Tucker's issue management models and behavioral frameworks sparked one highly regarded trade publication *The Holmes Report* (now called PRovoke) to name our firm the "best of niche." The report had this to say about Nuffer, Smith, Tucker: "The firm has a reputation for top-drawer strategic thinking... its issue management expertise is unrivaled on the West Coast... passionate implementation and unparalleled connections within its main area of expertise—the agri-food sector."

Tucker Tales

Howard Chase coined the term "issue management" and founded the discipline in 1976. He was a very thoughtful guy and an acknowledged contrarian by nature. So when I saw him standing in a lengthy line to talk to me following a presentation to the Issue Management Council in Washington, D.C., my brain immediately began retracing its steps for anything I might have said that could have upset the gentleman. Worst case, he could tell me and anyone in shouting distance that I was full of baloney. When he finally reached me, he said something to the effect of, "What you have presented is precisely how I've envisioned issue management working."

I only saw Howard one other time before he passed. I was to receive an award in his name. Chase himself presented it, citing our leadership in the field and published works.

Teresa and Blake's Take

The world is moving fast these days, and we are too. Our brains are on warp speed, which is a byproduct of our generation. In this whirlwind, it can be easy to forget to take a breath and strategically think about the future. While the suggestions here are important, so too is setting aside a little "me time" to truly think about and process what changes are happening around you and how best to act. Take the time to reach out to your personal and professional network. We have data all around us, but personal insight on a range of issues can be gained from a lunch date or by grabbing a drink with a valued friend or colleague to catch up on the important things going on in their lives. Being a good listener is a big part of the strategic planning process, so put it into practice regularly. Like other learnings in this book, Learning 3 can only be fully realized with thoughtfulness, presence, and space to think strategically and creatively.

Get to work: One shortcut for shaping change

These days, there are tools that aren't complicated or expensive for identifying issues. In fact, you may already be doing it.

1. For starters, do you have Google Alerts set up for your company using keywords for your business and clients? Do you have a media list that you and your staff scan daily for industry-relevant clips? Start a log of media coverage and start looking for themes. Every month or so, sit down with your planning team and go through them. If you are committed and dedicate the time, you will likely start to see threats and opportunities as they evolve, and you will be in a better position to make educated assumptions about which issues have the most influence on your purpose and vision and where these issues or trends are heading.

2. Choose a small group of thoughtful colleagues, and brainstorm issues likely to impact your organization's purpose and vision. Some helpful categories include economics, society, marketplace, technology, government. This group could dig deeper into each priority issue. Start by asking some key questions:

   a. What is the issue?
   b. Who's driving it?
   c. Who else is affected?
   d. What's their likely position and behavioral inclinations?
   e. Who is likely to support your organization or industry (or at least stay neutral)?
   f. Who is likely to oppose you?
   g. What's working for your organization or industry on the issue?
   h. What's working against you?
   i. Given all of this, how is the issue likely to play out and can your organization have a hand in shaping it?

Pick an issue important to your organization and use the questions above to draft a behavioral game plan.

Learning 4

Set a Clear Vision for the Future and a Plan to Fulfill It

"If you have more than five goals, you have none... If you want something new, you have to stop doing something old."
— Peter Drucker

By now, we hope you see the benefit of drilling down to uncover and utilize an organization's purpose and values, as well as setting up systems to anticipate, shape, and manage change. While these items are valuable, they do not stand on their own. Rather, to truly be successful, organizations must think more broadly about their future; this is what strategic planning is all about.

Strategic planning is about answering four basic questions:

1. Where are you now as an organization?

2. Where do you want to be?

3. How are you going to get there together?

4. How will you know when you have arrived?

Your first round of planning can be as basic as collecting as much intelligence as you can and asking these four questions of your management or planning team. That conversation alone can open the door to more strategic thinking.

For those considering more formal planning efforts, we know the term "strategic planning" can be bothersome and conjures up negative connotations. We also know negative experiences with strategic planning are painful and plentiful. Having acknowledged such, give it another name—perhaps a "visioning plan"—and move on to the important stuff: identifying the best strategic direction for your company, your trade association or community group.

A simple approach

The success of your planning is only as good as the intelligence you've collected, the process you're following, and the wisdom of the diversified planning team you've pulled together.

"True strategy is about placing bets and making hard choices," writes Roger L. Martin in the Harvard Business Review article "The Big Lie of Strategic Planning" (January–February 2014).

"[Good strategy is] the result of a simple and quite rough-and-ready process of thinking through what it will take to achieve what you want and then assessing whether it's realistic to try," said Martin.

Martin cites three rules:

1. Keep it simple.

2. Don't look for perfection.

3. Make the logic explicit—that is, be clear about what the company needs to do differently to reach its vision.

A thoughtful strategic-planning process is capable not only of setting up an organization for success and uncovering game-changing opportunities, but also of digging an organization out of the deepest of holes. You have to trust the process and not veer away from it at the first sign of discomfort or difficulty. Trust the process. Years of experience suggest it won't let you down.

There are two major functions to our Compass planning process. First, there's the "strategic" piece—clarifying where you want to head as an enterprise and how you intend to get there. Equally important but receiving far less attention is the "ownership" piece—getting stakeholders who are vital to the successful implementation to own and implement the plan.

Our four-step approach involves:

1. **Data collection**—This can include interviews, surveys, and other data collection to answer the question, "Where are you now?" During these inputs, participants are asked a series of questions about what they feel are the main threats and opportunities facing the organization. Nuffer, Smith, Tucker also gathers input on key components of the plan (purpose, vision, mission, values, and strengths and vulnerabilities of the organization). Interviews provide a foundation of themes, so planning sessions don't have to start from scratch.

2. **Planning workshop/retreat**—A planning workshop is then held to answer the question, "Where do you want to be?" Our facilitators can then come to the meeting with a workbook that includes candidates for key elements of the plan. At the conclusion of the planning session, the planning team comes to consensus on purpose, values, mission, priority external and internal issues, vision, and the strategic priorities to achieve the vision.

3. **Working group sessions**—Next, working groups get specific about action plans to answer the question: "How will we get there together?" This can happen at a second workshop involving a broader number of players or in small, offline sessions.

4. **Development of objectives/finalizing the plan**—Finally, teams develop the specific, measurable, achievable, relevant, and time-bound (SMART) objectives. Nuffer, Smith, Tucker then provides recommendations to ensure teams are aligned behind the plan and resources are in place to bring the plan to life.

We've found that having an agreed-upon vernacular is critical to gaining agreement on key planning elements. These are the definitions we use, and while your planning effort can use different terminology, it's important to have agreement on what each piece means and should do.

- Purpose: the highest benefit to people or society.

- Core values: principles that drive decision making.

- Mission: defines your core business.

- Vision: the destination you are working toward, e.g., your "man on the moon" or "Climb Mt. Everest" challenge.

- Strategic priorities: a handful of areas you focus on to achieve the vision.

- Envisioned future: a narrative of how success plays out in 1–2 pages.

- SMART objectives: specific, measurable, achievable, relevant, and time-bound measures of success developed for each strategic priority.

- Action plans: steps to be completed under each strategic priority.

Critical factors for success planning

- Partner involvement and commitment

- Decisions based on data (e.g., customer segments, community needs assessment)

- Clear focus on vision and priorities that leverage resources to make the biggest difference

- Measurable objectives

- The capability (human/financial) to carry out objectives

- Clear delineation of actions, responsibilities, and timelines

- Plan in written form and communicated widely (e.g., all stakeholders)

- Mechanism to evaluate progress and make adjustments

Figure 4: Critical factors for success planning

Writing "Smart" Objectives

S: Specific/Single outcome

M: Measurable

A: Achievable

R: Related/Reasonable

T: Time bound

Figure 5: Setting objectives

Tips for Action Planning

Preparing an Action Plan is just like making a list of tasks you want to accomplish in a day's work. The main differences are: more people involved; the timing is more precise; more information is provided; and it covers much more than one day's work.

The Action Plan form we recommend using is simple and well-proven. It starts with a heading at the top that spells out the wording of a specific Strategy. It also provides for stating the Priority involved and its Objective(s).

In our planning system, we need at least one Action Plan for each Strategy.

Next, under the column reading **ACTION STEPS**, list the major steps that must be taken to make implementation of the Strategy happen. These steps should be listed in the chronological sequence in which you believe they should be taken. They should be numbered. Each step should start with an action word (i.e., a verb).

It is not necessarily to become finely detailed in listing the steps. However, the steps should not be so broad, lumpy, or abstract in their language that we cannot later determine progress (or lack of progress) toward their completion.

Going on…for each Action Step we need to indicate who is responsible for doing it. This can be an organization unit or an individual. It is probable that in some steps more than one organization unit or individual who is responsible. Whatever the case, use the **WHO'S RESPONSIBLE** column to show the parties. If more than one individual has a shared responsibility, underline, boldface, or italicize the name of the most accountable person. You can use the **REMARKS** column to explain why this person is recommended to chair the joint effort.

For each step on the Action Plan form, there are three columns calling for dates. **STARTING DATE** means when a step should begin. **SCHEDULED COMPLETION DATE** is your recommended deadline for finishing the step. **ACTUAL COMPLETION DATE** will be used later to note when the step, in fact, has been completed.

The **REMARKS** column has many uses. The best Action Plans usually have many useful entries in this column.

REMEMBER

Participation is a key to successful implementation.

Consult with the organizations and individuals whom you believe should be responsible for taking action steps. Obtain their input. This is a bridge to gaining understanding, commitment and action.

OTHER TIPS

Keep in mind that an Action Plan is a plan. It is meant to lay out clearly and specifically things that have to be done in the future. However, when you are immersed in preparing one, it is easy to assume it is a report on things already done, putting yourself under unwarranted stress when looking ahead to the date the Action Plan will be presented. At this point in our process, we are still planning, not doing. The doing is implementation, and it comes later.

In preparing Action Plans be careful you do not start too many steps at the same time or too soon. Some Action Plans may not even have their initial steps scheduled for several months or in some cases, even in the first year of the strategic plan. If we try to do everything at once, we can set ourselves up for frustration and a sense of failure.

Figure 6: Tips for action planning

A closer look at Compass

A description of Compass—Nuffer, Smith, Tucker's strategic planning process—follows. The process is divided by strategy (Learning 4) and structure (Learning 5).

Compass strategy

I. External Assessment:

1. *Trends facing our society/industry/organization:*

- Analysis of macro trends data.

- Analysis of future industry-specific issues, trends, special events.

- Set priorities.

2. *Our marketplace:*

- Where are our key markets?

- How are they segmented?

- What are the sizes of each market?

- What are the trends influencing growth?

- Which markets offer the most growth potential?

3. *Our competition:*

- Who are our principal competitors?

- In what way(s) do we compete?

- How are our competitors perceived in the marketplace?

- Where are they strong?

- Where are they vulnerable?

- Where do we have competitive advantages?

- How do we position ourselves for the marketplace?

4. *Out-of-the-box futuristic scenarios to stretch thinking:*

- What's our worst nightmare?

- What's a description of a fundamentally different but better world?

II. Internal Assessment

1. *Who are we and what do we stand for?*

- Who is our customer? What needs do we meet?

- What's our mission, our core business?

- What unique benefits and services do we provide? What does society and people expect of our organization; our highest order or purpose?

- What are our core values? What do we stand for? What lies at the heart of consistent decision making and the behavioral expectations of management?

2. *Do management and staff live by these core values?*

3. *Our internal strengths and areas of vulnerability:*

- Internally, where are the organization's strengths, particularly those that may be underutilized?

- How important are our strengths to our customers?

- Where are our areas of vulnerability, especially those that will create major difficulty if not addressed?

- What data is available to draw assumptions (e.g., market and opinion research)? What additional information do we need (e.g., proprietary/secondary research)?

III. Vision/Positioning for the Future

1. *Our vision of success for the future:*

- How will we describe success at some time in the future (e.g., your moonshot or climbing Mount Everest "big hairy audacious goal" as coined by Jim Collins)?

2. *Our best positioning/differentiation/brand/or marketplace niche:*

- How are we perceived in the marketplace?

- What separates us from the competition?

- How would we like to be strategically positioned?

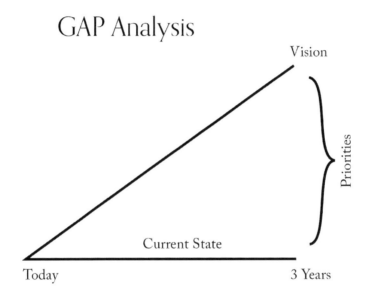

Today → Where are we now?
Vision → Where do we want to be?
Priorities → How are we going to get there <u>together?</u>

Figure 7: Gap analysis

IV. Compass Priorities

1. *Gap analysis/strategic priorities:*

- Is the organization aligned on strategic priorities? Is there misalignment? What are the obstacles to be overcome?

- Where are the major gaps between the current situation and our vision state? Where do we most need to do things that are new, better, and different to fulfill our core purpose, values, and vision?

- Where do we focus for major scores (vs. scratching at the surface or being satisfied with incremental change)?

- If we do all of this, will we achieve the vision?

2. *Develop measurable objectives and action plans for each priority.*

Action Plan

Strategic Priority:				
Objective:				
Strategy:				
Action Steps	Who Is Responsible	Scheduled Completion Date	Actual Completion Date	REMARKS (e.g., opportunities or problems uncovered; talents or weaknesses revealed; coordinated efforts required)
1.				
2.				
3.				
4.				
5.				
6.				
7.				

Figure 8: Sample action plan document

Tucker Tales

> *Looking over my career, I've been drawn to people with values similar to my own and a sense of humility that encourages checking egos at the door and giving multi-disciplined teams the freedom to craft solutions that evolve and build from collective inputs that no one individual is likely to develop on his/her own. Give me a mix of humble Golden Rule-type folks in the upper two percent of disciplines relevant to an organization, and we'll facilitate a strategy that has every possibility—with proper execution—of game-changing opportunities or resolving even the thorniest of problems. These are the folks we try to pull together on planning teams, and we encourage you to do so too.*

A closer look at Growers Express

It's important that everyone understands what vision (your destination) and your envisioned future (a one to two page narrative of how your vision plays out).

A common picture of success is important to bringing others on board with a clear understanding of what it is you're trying to accomplish. Consider this example from Growers Express:

> *"Growers Express is known as the next-generation healthful foods company, driven largely by the ambition of Jamie Strachan, who in early 2016—after gaining additional capital to support forward-thinking planning—helped propel the company forward and establish new mainstay categories in fresh and frozen vegetables.*

> *"The company is breathing new life into a mature and, at times, stale vegetable category, with retailers and consumers increasingly enthusiastic about fresh vegetables and innovation stemming from Growers Express. The company's strategic efforts are bringing a new, modern outlook at the*

retail and consumer level, securing its position in a rapidly changing industry.

"Retail formats are evolving, and suppliers and manufacturers need to make major adjustments toward revitalization to meet and succeed in this transitional environment. Growers Express is ahead of the game and thriving by offering on-trend solutions..

"Consumers continue to move away from processed foods and are now driven to prepare and consume whole foods and fresh produce. Led in large part by millennials who seek fresh, clean, simple, healthy, sustainable products, the 'Generation Next' movement (as Jamie has coined it) is also backed by their willingness to pay more for these high quality, pure products. Through its unique product offerings, Growers Express is not only exceeding consumers' growing expectations, it is sparking healthier lifestyles.

"With a shrinking commodity market, the company is building a branded fresh offering with the right product set. Innovations like Growers Express' trimmed and peeled Brussels sprouts products and the popular cauliflower rice and spiralized veggies have positively supported this effort. Because of these and a growing list of innovations and healthful and easy-to-use products that do not forego flavor and preserve the essence of the vegetables, the Green Giant Fresh brand is increasingly synonymous with the next generation of healthful eating.

"Success with the Green Giant Fresh innovations, including riced and spiralized vegetable categories, led the company to expand its strategy in support of B&G Foods to co-develop parallel offerings for Green Giant Frozen.

"Growers Express transitioned from a regional commodity vegetable company to being the largest grower processor of

riced cauliflower and spiralized vegetable products in North America, producing over a million consumer units weekly. Innovations in automation and mechanization have also increased efficiencies and added to the creation of the right infrastructure to meet needs.

"As a company focused on servicing retailers and consumers with healthy fare, the company led the way to delivering next generation healthful foods on a national scale and remains focused on its end goal: increasing the consumption of pure vegetables. By focusing on this goal, everyone benefits—from the farmers and employees to retailers, foodservice operators, and consumers. Serving all of these segments, while growing the category; regularly innovating new, on-trend products; building the brand; and continually offering the most premium, pure vegetable products in the marketplace is the new norm."

A closer look at National Pork Board

How might all the elements you learned about in this chapter come together? Remember, when creating your action plan make sure it is led by vision, its envisioned future and its major components. See the following pieces from the National Pork Board.

Vision

The National Pork Board will elevate U.S. pork as the global protein of choice by continuously and collaboratively working to do what's right for people, pigs, and the planet.

Mission

The National Pork Board is the catalyst that unites pork producers and key stakeholders focused on building a bright future for the pork industry through research, promotion, and education.

Values

- We value all diversity of opinion and strive for collaboration.
- We embrace the industry's "We Care" program; fulfilling our purpose of doing what's right—for people, pigs, and the planet.
- We are proactive in defining solutions for emerging challenges.
- We are committed to continuous improvement in all we do.

Strategic priorities

1. Build consumer trust.
2. Drive sustainable production.
3. Grow consumer demand.

Tucker Tales

Bob Smith understood the importance of doing homework before developing a strategic plan. He was a hoarder of process data. If you called him and asked for a refresher on Force Field Analysis (another strategy for issue analysis), he would drop whatever he was doing and pull out a document he'd written for this or that client. I learned from him to hold on tight to valuable information—you never know when it can be put to use later.

Teresa and Blake's Take

There are different perspectives on vision. Some, like us, prefer vision statements that can never truly be achieved. Other people like vision statements to be a little bit more within the realm of possibility. No matter your perspective, a vision statement should be big. It should also be well known by your team. Hang it up in your conference room, break room, or offices. A big vision statement can inspire big ideas.

Get to work: Rolling up your sleeves on a planning effort

Planning like anything else requires practice if you're going to excel. There's no better way than to "learn by doing." Just ask any good Cal Poly San Luis Obispo graduate, as that university has embraced this as its underlying philosophical principle. Reading about something only gets you so far. Acting on it? Now, that's where the learning starts to happen.

So, let's get started.

1. Pick your planning team. Be judicious but be diverse. Select individuals who can bring a unique perspective to the planning table.

2. Invest the time. Block one to two days on your calendar for strategic planning and stick with it.

3. Gather input in advance and come to the meeting with themes to use as a starting point for discussion.

4. If you need help, retain it. An experienced facilitator can get your strategic plan off the ground and give you an idea of how to run your own session next year.

5. If it gets too challenging, take a break. Walk away. Revisit the four key questions, and try again. Keep it simple.

6. Get team buy in. If you want your plan to succeed, everyone needs to be on the same page by the close of the planning session.

7. Assign responsibilities. Make your team owners of the plan and they are more likely to follow through, even champion the plan.

8. Set a timeline to evaluate the status of the plan. Make any necessary adjustments.

Learning 5

Align the Organization: Strategy, Culture, Infrastructure

*"If you could get all people rowing the same direction,
you can dominate any industry in any market against
any corporation at any given time."*
— *Patrick Lencioni, author of The Five Dysfunctions of a Team*

Think of alignment as everyone in your organization aiming for the same target. Aligning an organization behind the plan is as important as the plan itself.

A new strategic plan or the replenishment of an existing plan is a major undertaking for any company, trade association or not for profit community group. It's certainly not something you take lightly. At a minimum, it's a clarification of purpose and core values, vision and strategic priorities – and a tailoring of each job from top to bottom to maximize impact.

It's one thing to get a small planning team to line up behind a plan that they themselves developed and quite another to get middle managers and those who work for them to understand the direction management wants to head. This is where alignment comes into play.

Good to Great author Jim Collins simplifies the process of alignment into two steps: identify and correct misalignments and look for new opportunities to align. "It's a process of talking to people," says Collins. "If these are our core values and this is fundamentally why we exist [purpose] and this is our destination [vision], what are the obstacles that get in the way of aligning the organization behind the strategic plan?"

Most executives today know their enterprise should be aligned. They know their strategies, organizational capabilities, resources and management systems should be arranged to support the purpose of an organization. "The challenge is that executives tend to focus on one of these areas to the exclusion of the others, but what really matters for performance is how they fit together," says Jonathan Trevor and Barry Varcoe in Harvard Business Review (Feb. 27, 2017).

Alignment is a big deal, says Miles Reiter, CEO at Driscoll's Berry Company, the largest berry company in the world. "While our roots are in California and it is by far our most lucrative business unit, we treat our three business units alike (America, Africa and Asia Pacific), and there is no pecking order. If we expect to achieve our vision of becoming the world's berry company's enriching the lives of those we touch every day, we have to be aligned across the company from top to bottom and left to right. Former Ocean Mist president, Joe Pezzini, led an organizational alignment strategy that merged the firm's premium vegetable messaging with its core values and competitive advantages.

There are at least four paths that can be used to align the organization behind the strategic plan.

1. Share the strategic plan with employees and other stakeholders.

- How well is the company aligned behind the strategic plan?

- Is there misalignment? How do we better align?

2. Assess the organization culture.

- How do company values and behavioral norms support the plan?

- What will it take to improve understanding and create ownership in the plan?

3. Provide a supportive infrastructure.

- Are we structured in the most effective and efficient way?
- Do we have the right people? Can we get them?
- What training will be in place?
- What technology support is needed?
- Do we have the resources to do what we need to do?
- How well aligned is the infrastructure?

4. Communicate progress against the plan.

- How will we share progress against the plan? (e.g. quarterly/monthly)

Share the strategic plan with employees and other stakeholders.

Ask yourself: Are employees likely to support it? Will they be likely to oppose it? Are there people who will need a rationale for supporting the plan? Will training be needed? You can't align an organization without engaging employees in at least understanding the direction you want to take the company and helping them determine their role in taking you there. In an era of fierce competition and the challenges of differentiating a business, we've found alignment to be the closest thing we know of to an internal competitive advantage.

Internal teams should be tasked to continually reference back to the strategic plan and tie tactics to the priorities. Often, teams may find themselves wondering if they should be pursuing particular actions, strategies, or tactics. For guidance, they should turn to the strategic plan. If an activity does not support the vision and a priority item, then it likely shouldn't be considered.

As leaders, you also have the opportunity to continually reinforce the plan. This can occur in numerous ways from quarterly check-in meetings, where reports are given on progress against the plan, to using the plan as the foundation for setting agendas for internal meetings. For some Nuffer, Smith, Tucker clients, board-meeting agendas are set up in alignment with strategic priorities.

Leaders also have an opportunity to put values front and center by talking about them often and having them prominently displayed. In addition, one should not overlook the importance of the strategic plan (and the values in particular) in the hiring process. At Nuffer, Smith, Tucker, values are shown to prospective employee candidates, who are then asked to explain their interpretation of the values and talk about which appeal most to them.

There are numerous ways to involve your team in the planning process. This includes:

- Survey and/or personally interview key employees.

- Work with your team to paint a picture of success. Ask them to brainstorm what success will look like and create a narrative of this picture.

- Share a preliminary draft of the strategic plan with key employees for feedback and buy in.

- Involve staff in building out SMART objectives and action plans they are responsible for in support of the plan.

- Provide formal training where needed to implement the plan.

- Hold briefings with staff, allowing for questions and answers and tweaks that help shape the plan and foster ownership.

- Help employees personalize key planning components (e.g., values, purpose, mission, vision, strategic priorities) to their own jobs. For example, have them break up into small groups and ask: What do the core values mean to you? What do you need to do differently to live them? What do we/you need to stop doing? Where do we/you focus to make the biggest difference in living your company values?

Assess the organization culture.

"Culture is the implicit, informal potent system of norms in an enterprise," wrote Bob Smith. "Culture is defined as the environment and climate created by the key values we believe in…and the behavior and performance which are rewarded and punished."

It's often said that culture trumps strategy every time. Your people are that important. Their support is everything. Whether or not culture is more important than strategy is a moot point. The reality is that you need both strategy and culture (along with infrastructure) to maximize success. Employees can be a force to reckon with if they don't feel listened to, involved, engaged or part of the team working on moving beyond the status quo. Culture can be a powerful force in adding value to a direction management wants to take if employees are in sync and on board. Engaging and inspiring a multi-generational mix of employees is the challenge, and culture has tremendous influence on the employee population.

What's it like to work within your organization? Assess what it takes to be successful in a culture?. Does your organization have the values, beliefs, and behaviors in place to create a positive culture? Does it need help? If so, what needs improving? How can you adjust current plans to support the new direction without losing traction on existing planning priorities?

Provide a supportive infrastructure.

The third pathway deals with infrastructure: How do you organize your people for greater effectiveness and efficiencies? What resources and operational systems—human, technology, and financial—are available?

Revising an organization's infrastructure is often seen as a way to improve efficiency, promote teamwork, create synergy, or reduce cost," says Don Shapiro, president of First Concepts Consultants, Inc. When a company makes major changes, it must carefully think through every aspect of the structure required to support the strategy. And while the first thing many people think of when they hear "structure" is an organizational chart, infrastructure should be thought of more broadly.

A Sample Organization Chart

```
                    ┌─────────────────┐
                    │      CEO        │
                    └─────────────────┘
         ┌───────────────┼───────────────┐
┌─────────────────┐ ┌─────────────────┐ ┌─────────────────┐
│ Vice President  │ │ Vice President  │ │ Director Human  │
│    Finance      │ │  Manufacturing  │ │   Resources     │
└─────────────────┘ └─────────────────┘ └─────────────────┘
┌─────────────────┐ ┌─────────────────┐ ┌─────────────────┐
│     Chief       │ │     Plant       │ │   Training      │
│   Accountant    │ │ Superintendent  │ │   Specialist    │
└─────────────────┘ └─────────────────┘ └─────────────────┘
┌─────────────────┐ ┌─────────────────┐ ┌─────────────────┐
│     Budget      │ │   Maintenance   │ │   Benefits      │
│     Analyst     │ │ Superintendent  │ │  Administrator  │
└─────────────────┘ └─────────────────┘ └─────────────────┘
```

Figure 9: A functional or bureaucratic model of organization

Businesses use organization charts to clarify responsibility and define hierarchy within an enterprise. Structure can divide an organization by function (e.g., marketing, finance), by division (e.g., products and services), by matrix (e.g., projects and/or jobs with multiple bosses), even organized by strategy.

The state of the culture of an organization rarely receives the influence it deserves given its importance to the success or failure of the strategic plan.

The questions then become, do you have the right people in the right chairs, and the right culture and infrastructure in place to support your plan.

"We view infrastructure as including the people, support systems (like technology), and resources needed to implement the strategic plan. While some organizations look at structure in the context of continuous improvement or 'efficiencies,' the best time to look at this area is after a strategic plan is developed," says Shapiro. If there's no strategic plan, how do you know if you are organized well enough to implement it?

It's just not enough to assume that people will leap over tall buildings to understand, get excited about, and support a new strategic direction—let alone own it. Take our assessment at the end of this learning to put your finger on the pulse of your organization. Like what you see? Great. If not, it's time to invest in building the culture you want and need.

Communicate progress against the plan.

Ask yourself: What's our plan for communicating the plan to key constituents? Who needs to be informed? What information do we share with whom? Have we clearly shared our direction and rationale for change? How frequently do we share progress, collect feedback, and incorporate it into the planning process?

It's important that members of an industry board of directors embrace an organization's values and culture. Richard Waycott, CEO of the Almond Board of California points to a food safety outbreak linked to almonds in 2004 as an example of the board's forward looking culture. Pasteurization was a bold move to shore up the industry's safety vulnerability for a lot of reasons. "Our board helped us with the third party expertise and gave them full authority to accelerate the redesign of our production systems," says Waycott.

A closer look at the dairy groups

In the early 1990s, Cynthia Carson, CEO of the National Dairy Board, was hired with a mandate to organize the industry's $200 million investment in promotion behind a common marketing vision and strategic plan. Up until that point, there were two national promotion groups—National Dairy Board and United Dairy Industry Association—with two separate campaigns. There were also several regional promotion groups with minimal coordination of industry resources. Carson retained Nuffer, Smith, Tucker to design and lead a strategic planning process, beginning with the formation of an industry-wide planning team to gain consensus on a set of industry core values to drive planning decisions, develop a mission for the organization, and create a vision to define success with a set of industry-wide strategic priorities to achieve that vision.

Pulling the dairy industry together was a feat far easier said than done, given the political underbelly of the country's dairy industry. The year-long process seemed to take two steps backward for every step forward, but Carson's tenacity and support from industry leaders pushed the process forward. The benefits of one industry-wide marketing strategy and strategic plan were undeniable.

On the California front, as you read in earlier learnings, Dairy Council of California is a purpose-driven organization. The organization uses the term "cause" to define what really drives them: elevating the health of children and families. While this cause is at the organization's core and passion of the staff and board, there was a time when it wasn't always so front and center. This changed with now-CEO Tammy Anderson-Wise.

Anderson-Wise saw firsthand the magnetic pull of aligning behind their cause and what the cause did to spark employee and stakeholder engagement. The difference in employee morale alone shot new life into a culture struggling to meet the ambitious demands of the industry.

"A few years ago, asking an employee to recite the mission of the organization drew blank stares and foiled attempts," said Anderson-Wise. "Today, there's no one in the organization who cannot at least parrot the cause: elevating the health of children and families through the pursuit of lifelong healthy eating patterns."

Anderson-Wise recognized that alignment doesn't happen by accident. Over time, she has invested in board and staff training, formally assessed the culture, and targeted areas for improvement. She also recreated the organizational structure to better support alignment and implementation of the success plan. The end result is that everyone in the organization, from administrative professionals to board members, is now aligned to clearly see how she/he fits individually and collectively into the future of Dairy Council of California and the impacts it strives to achieve.

Engaging employees at all levels of the planning process is the big idea here., The days of taking employees for granted are all but over. "Alignment is the glue to performance excellence," writes Jackie Tucker Gangnes in "Thought Exchange." "When alignment is off, your boat strays off course – wasting time, energy and resources." This is true for growing teams and is certainly true for you. Flexibility is the new currency in the workplace for employees and employers.

"After a tried and tested period of uncertainty and relentless change, the ability to be nimble, agile and resilient for our future world is more than essential – it's expected, writes Tucker Gangnes." Employees expect and seek greater flexibility to allow more work life balance.

Teresa and Blake's Take

> Have you ever walked into an office or other environment that just feels heavy? Maybe you got the sense that people don't want to be there? Or maybe it is eerily quiet? If your team doesn't want to be there, it will eventually become obvious to anyone who steps through the door. (The movie Office Space may come to mind.) Collaboration, camaraderie, and, ultimately, client relations and work product will suffer. On the flip side, some organizations are filled with an energy that is palpable. People are engaged, filled with purpose, and understand the future direction of the organization and their role in it. This is the type of organization we seek to build at Nuffer, Smith, Tucker and the types of organizations we want to work with. For this to happen, all the learnings here need to come together. The end result is nothing short of magic.

Get to work: Assessing your organization's culture

You can do your own preliminary assessment of your company culture by seeking answers to the battery of questions that follow and writing a brief narrative of "what it's like to work at your organization." If you find it to be a useful tool, have your management team and a sample of employees do a similar exercise. Compare and contrast. You'll likely get close to an accurate assessment of your culture. You can also assign a "champion" to more formally assess your company culture and any misalignments with the strategic plan that need attention.

Communication

- Who talks to whom?

- How frequently is communication happening between team members and cross functionally?

- How often does leadership address and engage the team and in what ways?

- Is communication straightforward and candid or do people need to read between the lines?

Recognition

- Who gets recognized and rewarded?

- Who gets ignored and punished?

- What do people do to get ahead?

- What do people do to stay out of trouble?

  - How do decisions get made?
  - How are newcomers treated?

- How are ex-officers and staff treated?

- Do people get shot at sunrise if they make a mistake?

- Can people get emotional and still be respected?
- Do they kill the messenger?
- How would you describe the level of trust within the organization?

Rites and rituals

- Are there special, even beloved rites and rituals?
- Are there respected heroes and heroines?
- Are there myths and legends?

Culture

- Is the culture orderly or disorganized?
- Does the culture have a short-term or long-term orientation?
- How do decisions get made?
- Is there too much attention on internal stuff at the expense of dealing with the outside world?
- How would you describe the level of trust within the organization?
- Are your organization's values explicit and out in the open?
- Do management and staff live by them?
- What behaviors do these values demand?
- What as an organization do you need to stop doing to assure these values drive decisions?
- Are there new and different behaviors needed to assure these values become part of your organization's culture?

Learning 6

One Leader's Journey: Thriving Personally and Professionally

*"We can talk about making a difference
or we can make a difference."*
— Anonymous

Case Study: Tim York and Markon Cooperative

Our friend and long-time client Tim York took everything we've been talking about in this book and put it to work. His story is proof of how our process can get you there.

York introduced himself to the Nuffer, Smith, Tucker team in the early 1990s in the lobby of the Carmel Valley Inn, just east of Monterey. We were leading a strategic planning retreat for the board of directors of the Produce Marketing Association, the trade group for buyers and sellers of fresh produce. We were out the door headed for a taxi when Tim caught up to us and asked if we needed a lift to the airport.

Little did we know this cordial conversation would result in more than three decades of working together on strategic advantage, shrewd market leadership, and dabbling now and again in managing, even shaping, change.

Tim and his team broadly pursued new opportunities improve consumption and differentiate Markon, a produce purchasing cooperative, including new strategies to re-imagine the produce experience for its members. The team also dug into the creation of sustainable products and practices and has explored solutions on managing food waste.

If you know anyone in the produce business, they're likely to know the story of Markon. Tim is one of a few visible leaders in produce. He's a columnist for *The Packer*, the fresh fruit and vegetable industry's leading source for news since 1893. His views are sought out by peers. People pay attention to him, which is likely the reason he was hired as CEO of the Leafy Green Marketing Agreement, whose purpose is to manage food safety for leafy greens..

The running commentary that follows describes how York implemented the five learnings from this book at Markon to make a difference.

Learning One: Focus on purpose to make a difference

One of the greatest motivators for the Markon team is knowing the organization stands for more than the almighty dollar; that confidence in every box of product is more than just a talking point in a sales flyer. Tim lives Learning One clear as the day is long—running a purposeful enterprise and recognizing that bringing safe food to market is of unmatched importance.

Under Tim's leadership, Markon was among the first companies to respond strategically in 1998 to the initiation of food safety requirements for brand suppliers. A year later, they introduced their branded Five Star Food Safety program. By 2002, all suppliers were required to have at a minimum a third-party passing grade on its food safety audit. By 2004, Markon eliminated twenty-five percent of its suppliers because they had no foundational food safety program. Markon's food safety credentials gave it credibility and a point of differentiation. With its seriousness as a public health issue rising by the day, they began to consider the pros and cons of safety as a pre-competitive industry issue. That is, the industry is only as good as its weakest link, and when trouble strikes, the entire category is negatively affected.

An *E. coli*-tainted spinach outbreak in 2006, resulting in illness and death, brought the produce industry to its knees. Markon was uniquely positioned to take the lead on food safety during this time, and it did. York organized major buyers to mandate a system for leafy greens with very specific protocol trace-back and marketplace procedures. The loose-knit collaboration of retail and foodservice buyers encouraged the produce trade groups to accelerate the development of a new set of industry-wide standards. Markon was able to facilitate collective changes due to the power of its purchasing decisions.

Tim is carrying over the notion of purpose to LGMA, where he will continue to advocate for determining why and how foodborne illness continues to be a vulnerability.

Learning Two: Living by values

While many of the purpose-led initiatives were spearheaded by York, the values at Markon live at every level of the organization, as it advocates for Learning Two. If Markon did nothing but live its core values, it would be a company ahead of the game in terms of strategic thinking.

Tim surrounds himself with hard-working produce veterans, young and old, who share Markon's view of the world and know how to run a successful produce company. Markon's hiring practices over the years have been guided by York's ability to size up how a candidate is likely to fit the company's core values, purpose, vision and mission.

Employees are expected to live these values and are encouraged to call out those who don't.

Markon core values include:

- People matter.

- Do the right thing.

- Innovate.

- Create confidence in every case.

Learning Three: Anticipating, managing, and shaping change

Systems to anticipate, manage, and even shape change are the lifeline of Nuffer, Smith, Tucker and engaged clients like Markon. Most of us handle issues instinctively, almost accidentally—or we wait until they become crises. While food safety has been at the heart of Markon for some time, York didn't stop there. Through his ongoing efforts to evaluate forces working for and against Markon and the industry, York identified food waste as priority issue.

York approached several food banks, the Feeding America organization and the California Association of Food Banks, to learn about their needs and challenges. Markon teamed with Steve Kenfield of HMC Farms, a table grape and tree fruit grower-shipper in California, on a promising idea to increase food bank contributions and foster greater efficiencies. Through these efforts, Tim shows that he has not just identified an issue or a challenge, but has developed ideas on possible solutions and taken action on those ideas.

Learning Four: Creating a clear vision

Every organization wants to be needed, valued, and an integral part of the world to those who interact with it. It's this essence that was embraced when Markon adopted a bold new vision: be indispensable.

While there are only two words in the statement, the meaning is big. It's a stretch goal that is not easily achieved. To ensure the vision was well understood, the company underwent a visioning exercise, thinking through and articulating on paper what the vision means and what it would look like if the vision was achieved. Importantly, Markon didn't just decide on that vision and go about its business. Instead, it aligned the entire organization behind the vision.

Learning Five: Aligning the organization behind the plan

Alignment is where we make the biggest difference in creating an understanding of, and support for, the strategic plan and its implementation. Alignment for Markon starts with the Salinas Management

Group and extends outward to fieldworkers inspecting and procuring product. Aligning the board and the produce managers of each owner's company is also critical to keeping owner companies involved and supportive of whatever plans are in the works. Alignment can come easier at a place like Markon because plans are built on the company's deep-seeded values.

Do it all again

Tim recently became the new CEO of LGMA, a group he helped create. In that role, he—like readers of this book—has the opportunity to take the lessons learned here and from the past and apply them to the future. By doing so, he and others will find that life and business is about more than simply checking in and checking out. It's about making a difference through purpose, values, shaping change, and building the future you want for yourself or your business.

Epilogue

Why did you pick up this book? Curiosity? In many ways, we're suggesting ramping up the anticipation and the shaping of change with systems we've successfully used for decades.

The pace of change continues to accelerate exponentially, and every issue, big and small, begs for attention. The noise alone can seduce you into allocating limited resources to the wrong employees, investors, neighbors, and customers—areas or pathways that aren't necessarily strategic to your success over the long haul. This can lead to distractions, unintended consequences, missed opportunities, misreading of red flags, and/or taking action on a single issue only to find your action negatively affecting other issues.

While sorting out priorities has been a key part of strategic planning since the early 1990s and before, we're certainly seeing a shift in the demand by our clientele to at least consider a commitment to restoring public trust as a potential planning priority. An optimal future depends on the ability of each business to get crystal clear on purpose, values, and a vision of success for the future.

Over a span of five decades, a foundation has been laid at Nuffer, Smith, Tucker of corporate values anchored by our commitment to grow our people and provide organizational support for the communities in which we work. Think about the strength of the purpose and values you've discovered. Does it give you the consistent identity Collins and Porras called for in 1996? Based on what you know today, do your purpose and core values give you a footing strong enough to successfully build a future for your organization? If you're not convinced, you may want to dig deeper.

Prosperity is recognizing the door is opening for people who have the courage to invest, including Cynthia Carson, Bill Even, Richard Waycott, Chris Novak, Arnott Duncan, Jamie Strachan, Jamie Johnson, Al Montna, John and Gail Kautz, Glen Broom, and my life-long partner, Linda Tucker. These are the individuals committed to thoughtful and creative decision making. The members will only grow, and the wisdom will be rewarded with financial support. That you can count on. Oh, and add Kerry Tucker, Teresa Siles, and Blake Tucker Nelson to your list.

Business is about more than simply checking in and checking out. It's about making a difference through purpose, values, shaping change, and building the future you want for yourself and your business.

About the Authors

Advising Nuffer, Smith, Tucker, Inc. since 1980, Kerry Tucker loves all things strategy and has spent most of his professional life helping companies decide what they want to be when they grow up. His book *Public Relations Writing: An Issue-Driven Behavioral Approach* (1989, 1994, 1997) has been adopted by hundreds of colleges and universities all over the world. Kerry also co-founded *Food Foresight*, a trends intelligence system for the agri-food chain and served on a number of university boards. He has won the W. Howard Chase Award, created by the Issue Management Council to recognize organizational excellence in issue management, as well as the Otto Bos Lifetime Achievement Award from the Public Relations Society of America, San Diego Chapter. Kerry lives in San Diego, CA.

Teresa Siles is president and partner of Nuffer, Smith, Tucker, Inc. She graduated from San Diego State University with a bachelor's degree in 2003 and an MBA in 2013. She is currently based in San Diego CA.

Blake Tucker Nelson, Kerry Tucker's daughter, runs My Sage PR, a boutique public affairs firm in Carlsbad, CA.

Printed in Canada